A PRAYER FOR YOU

Dear God, I pray for my dear brother or sister who is now using this book. I pray that their desire to seek you more deeply leads them to find you in the most amazing of ways. I pray that distractions be removed so that your still small voice would be incredibly clear. I pray that deep revelations and intimate realizations of you are consistently experienced as they pray over these next 90 days. God have your way in their prayer life and in their life in general. I come into agreement with them through prayer as they bring to you every concern, every grief, every pain, and every hope. May every desire that is within your will be made known to them as we trust your ways, your timing, and judgment. God, I pray that this person will enter a season of abundance within their life. As they heal, grow, and transform in you, I pray that they experience improved physical health, mental health, emotional health, spiritual health, and financial health. May the testimonies that come from this season show others that you are an incredible God. Finally, God, I pray that no weapon that is formed against them prospers. I pray that fear never overtakes them, as they remember that you are the God who fights with them and for them. May they stay hidden under your protection and guided by your divine direction.

in Jesus' name, I pray, Amen

Maurice J. Martin

PRAYER LIST

IF TWO OF YOU AGREE ON EARTH CONCERNING ANYTHING THAT THEY ASK,
IT WILL BE DONE FOR THEM BY MY FATHER IN HEAVEN" (MATT. 18:19)

NAME	PRAYER POINTS

PRAYER LIST

IF TWO OF YOU AGREE ON EARTH CONCERNING ANYTHING THAT THEY ASK,
IT WILL BE DONE FOR THEM BY MY FATHER IN HEAVEN" (MATT. 18:19)

NAME	PRAYER POINTS

ANSWERED PRAYERS

I PRAY WITH GREAT FAITH FOR YOU, BECAUSE I'M FULLY CONVINCED THAT THE ONE WHO BEGAN THIS GRACIOUS WORK IN YOU WILL FAITHFULLY CONTINUE THE PROCESS OF MATURING YOU UNTIL THE UNVEILING OF OUR LORD JESUS CHRIST! | PHILIPPIANS 1:6

DATE   PRAYER THAT WAS ANSWERED

_____   _____

_____   _____

_____   _____

_____   _____

_____   _____

_____   _____

_____   _____

_____   _____

_____   _____

_____   _____

_____   _____

_____   _____

ANSWERED PRAYERS

I PRAY WITH GREAT FAITH FOR YOU, BECAUSE I'M FULLY CONVINCED THAT THE ONE WHO
BEGAN THIS GRACIOUS WORK IN YOU WILL FAITHFULLY CONTINUE THE PROCESS OF
MATURING YOU UNTIL THE UNVEILING OF OUR LORD JESUS CHRIST! | **PHILIPPIANS 1:6**

DATE

PRAYER THAT WAS ANSWERED

PRAYER FOR PEACE

Dad, I lift up my brother/sister in prayer. I know that you have an unparalleled heart and a love for them. I pray that you could remind them that you are in control and that everything they need in this day is in your hands and your control. I pray, God, that they could pray to you according to Philippians 4:6-8. May they pray to you with openness, honesty, and transparency from the deepest place they can find within. After sharing their concerns, fears, and desires with you, I pray that you can help them find gratitude in their heart. May that process bring forth the peace of God that you assured them in your Word, that defies understanding. Peace in the midst of the storm. Peace in the midst of the facts and the details of the situation. Peace despite what they feel. Peace, because you are God and you are greater than any problem they face.

In Jesus' name, I pray

PRAYER FOR WISDOM

Heavenly Father, I come into agreement with my brother/sister seeking your divine Wisdom. God your word tells us in James 1:5-7 that you freely give wisdom, without judgment, when we come to you for it. I pray right now that you would release revelation, insight, and a healthy perspective to my brother/sister. I pray that they pursue mental and emotional healing with you. May that process remove every lie, every bit of confusion, and break every word curse that looks to disrupt or distort their perception. God, please give them eyes to see and ears to hear the Truth. Not the "truth" that the world offers, but Truth that comes only through you.

In Jesus' name, I pray

PRAYER FOR COMFORT

Dad, I come to you today with my brother/sister as they seek comfort from you. I don't know what is troubling them today, but you know God. You say in your Word in Matthew 5:4 that you send your Spirit to comfort those who mourn. You also say in Matthew 11:28-30 that people who are bearing a burden can go to you and that you can give them rest for their soul. I pray today God that my brother/sister has the courage to surrender every issue and release every weight into your loving arms. I pray that they would be comforted by you in a way that eases every stress, every strain, and every struggle. May they find rest with you on this day. I pray that your ministering angels surround them and they encounter your Spirit in a truly comforting and transcendent way right now. May you shift their atmosphere and touch their heart.

In Jesus' name, I pray

PRAYER FOR PROTECTION

Heavenly Father, I come to you in prayer right now with my brother/sister. This is your child whom you know and love. I stand in agreement with them right now in prayer as they pray for divine protection on this day. I pray that they would dwell and be protected by your presence, as your word invites us to do in Psalm 91. In that safe place, may they take comfort in knowing that they need not fight any battles on their own. God, we know that you are a good Father who goes ahead of us in battle and fights on our behalf. God, would you send your angels to provide divine protection for this situation they are facing? I pray that no weapon that forms prospers and that you would keep them from falling or stumbling today.

In Jesus' name, I pray

DAILY JOURNAL PROMPT

What do you want to thank God for today?

Is there anything troubling you that is disrupting your level of hope or your faith today?

What scripture will you focus on as a reminder of God's promises?

What do you sense God wants for you to remember or know today?

JEREMIAH 29:11

FOR I KNOW THE PLANS I HAVE FOR YOU, DECLARES THE LORD, PLANS TO PROSPER
YOU AND NOT TO HARM YOU, PLANS TO GIVE YOU HOPE AND A FUTURE.

DAILY JOURNAL PROMPT

What do you feel most
thankful for today?

Are there any issues that are
troubling you where you need
God's serenity?

What do you need God's
courage and strength to
change today?

What wisdom do you sense
God is attempting to share
with you or remind you of
today?

PSALM 118:4

THE LORD IS MY STRENGTH AND MY DEFENSE ; HE HAS BECOME MY SALVATION.

DAILY JOURNAL PROMPT

What do you want to thank God for today?

Is there anything troubling you that is disrupting your level of hope or your faith today?

What scripture will you focus on as a reminder of God's promises?

What do you sense God wants for you to remember or know today?

PSALM 42:11

WHY, MY SOUL, ARE YOU DOWNCAST? WHY SO DISTURBED WITHIN ME? PUT
YOUR HOPE IN GOD, OR I WILL YET PRAISE HIM, MY SAVIOR AND MY GOD.

DAILY JOURNAL PROMPT

What do you feel most
thankful for today?

Are there any issues that are
troubling you where you need
God's serenity?

What do you need God's
courage and strength to
change today?

What wisdom do you sense
God is attempting to share
with you or remind you of
today?

DANIEL 10:19

DO NOT BE AFRAID, YOU WHO ARE HIGHLY ESTEEMED," HE SAID. "PEACE! BE
STRONG NOW; BE STRONG." WHEN HE SPOKE TO ME, I WAS STRENGTHENED
AND SAID, "SPEAK. MY LORD, SINCE YOU HAVE GIVEN ME STRENGTH.

DAILY JOURNAL PROMPT

What do you want to
thank God for today?

Is there anything troubling you
that is disrupting your level of
hope or your faith today?

What scripture will you
focus on as a reminder of
God's promises?

What do you sense God
wants for you to remember
or know today?

ROMANS 15:13

MAY THE GOD OF HOPE FILL YOU WITH ALL JOY AND PEACE AS YOU TRUST IN HIM,
SO THAT YOU MAY OVERFLOW WITH HOPE BY THE POWER OF THE HOLY SPIRIT.

DAILY JOURNAL PROMPT

What do you feel most
thankful for today?

Are there any issues that are
troubling you where you need
God's serenity?

What do you need God's
courage and strength to
change today?

What wisdom do you sense
God is attempting to share
with you or remind you of
today?

PSALM 46:1
GOD IS OUR REFUGE AND STRENGTH, AN EVER-PRESENT HELP IN TROUBLE.

DAILY JOURNAL PROMPT

What do you want to
thank God for today?

Is there anything troubling you
that is disrupting your level of
hope or your faith today?

What scripture will you
focus on as a reminder of
God's promises?

What do you sense God
wants for you to remember
or know today?

HEBREWS 12:14

MAKE EVERY EFFORT TO LIVE IN PEACE WITH EVERYONE AND TO BE HOLY; WITHOUT HOLINESS NO ONE WILL SEE THE LORD.

DAILY JOURNAL PROMPT

What do you feel most
thankful for today?

Are there any issues that are
troubling you where you need
God's serenity?

What do you need God's
courage and strength to
change today?

What wisdom do you sense
God is attempting to share
with you or remind you of
today?

EPHESIANS 4:4

THERE IS ONE BODY AND ONE SPIRIT, JUST AS YOU WERE CALLED TO ONE HOPE WHEN YOU WERE CALLED.

DAILY JOURNAL PROMPT

What do you want to
thank God for today?

Is there anything troubling you
that is disrupting your level of
hope or your faith today?

What scripture will you
focus on as a reminder of
God's promises?

What do you sense God
wants for you to remember
or know today?

GALATIANS 5:22

BUT THE FRUIT OF THE SPIRIT IS LOVE, JOY, PEACE, FORBEARANCE, KINDNESS, GOODNESS, FAITHFULNESS,

DAILY JOURNAL PROMPT

What do you feel most
thankful for today?

Are there any issues that are
troubling you where you need
God's serenity?

What do you need God's
courage and strength to
change today?

What wisdom do you sense
God is attempting to share
with you or remind you of
today?

MICAH 7:7

BUT AS FOR ME, I WATCH IN HOPE FOR THE LORD.
I WAIT FOR GOD MY SAVIOR; MY GOD WILL HEAR ME.

DAILY JOURNAL PROMPT

What do you want to thank God for today?	Is there anything troubling you that is disrupting your level of hope or your faith today?
What scripture will you focus on as a reminder of God's promises?	What do you sense God wants for you to remember or know today?

PSALM 25:5

GUIDE ME IN YOUR TRUTH AND TEACH ME,
FOR YOU ARE GOD MY SAVIOR,
AND MY HOPE IS IN YOU ALL DAY LONG.

DAILY JOURNAL PROMPT

What do you feel most
thankful for today?

Are there any issues that are
troubling you where you need
God's serenity?

What do you need God's
courage and strength to
change today?

What wisdom do you sense
God is attempting to share
with you or remind you of
today?

PSALM 73:26

MY FLESH AND MY HEART MAY FAIL, BUT GOD IS THE
STRENGTH OF MY HEART AND MY PORTION FOREVER.

DAILY JOURNAL PROMPT

What do you want to thank God for today?

Is there anything troubling you that is disrupting your level of hope or your faith today?

What scripture will you focus on as a reminder of God's promises?

What do you sense God wants for you to remember or know today?

PSALM 106:8

NEVERTHELESS HE SAVED THEM FOR THE SAKE OF HIS NAME,
THAT HE MIGHT MAKE HIS POWER KNOWN.

DAILY JOURNAL PROMPT

What do you feel most
thankful for today?

Are there any issues that are
troubling you where you need
God's serenity?

What do you need God's
courage and strength to
change today?

What wisdom do you sense
God is attempting to share
with you or remind you of
today?

1 CORINTHIANS 10:13

NO TEMPTATION HAS OVERTAKEN YOU EXCEPT WHAT IS COMMON TO MANKIND. AND GOD IS
FAITHFUL; HE WILL NOT LET YOU BE TEMPTED BEYOND WHAT YOU CAN BEAR. BUT WHEN YOU
ARE TEMPTED, HE WILL ALSO PROVIDE A WAY OUT SO THAT YOU CAN ENDURE IT.

DAILY JOURNAL PROMPT

What do you want to thank God for today?

Is there anything troubling you that is disrupting your level of hope or your faith today?

What scripture will you focus on as a reminder of God's promises?

What do you sense God wants for you to remember or know today?

EXODUS 14:13

AND MOSES SAID TO THE PEOPLE, "FEAR NOT, STAND FIRM, AND SEE THE SALVATION OF THE LORD,
WHICH HE WILL WORK FOR YOU TODAY. FOR THE EGYPTIANS WHOM YOU SEE TODAY, YOU SHALL
NEVER SEE AGAIN."

DAILY JOURNAL PROMPT

What do you feel most
thankful for today?

Are there any issues that are
troubling you where you need
God's serenity?

What do you need God's
courage and strength to
change today?

What wisdom do you sense
God is attempting to share
with you or remind you of
today?

ROMANS 8:28

AND WE KNOW THAT IN ALL THINGS GOD WORKS FOR THE GOOD OF THOSE
WHO LOVE HIM, WHO HAVE BEEN CALLED ACCORDING TO HIS PURPOSE.

DAILY JOURNAL PROMPT

What do you want to thank God for today?

Is there anything troubling you that is disrupting your level of hope or your faith today?

What scripture will you focus on as a reminder of God's promises?

What do you sense God wants for you to remember or know today?

PHILIPPIANS 4:6-7

DO NOT BE ANXIOUS ABOUT ANYTHING, BUT IN EVERY SITUATION, BY PRAYER AND PETITION, WITH
THANKSGIVING, PRESENT YOUR REQUESTS TO GOD. AND THE PEACE OF GOD, WHICH TRANSCENDS
ALL UNDERSTANDING, WILL GUARD YOUR HEARTS AND YOUR MINDS IN CHRIST JESUS.

DAILY JOURNAL PROMPT

What do you feel most
thankful for today?

Are there any issues that are
troubling you where you need
God's serenity?

What do you need God's
courage and strength to
change today?

What wisdom do you sense
God is attempting to share
with you or remind you of
today?

2 CORINTHIANS 13:11

FINALLY, BROTHERS AND SISTERS, REJOICE! STRIVE FOR FULL RESTORATION, ENCOURAGE ONE ANOTHER. BE OF ONE MIND, LIVE IN PEACE. AND THE GOD OF LOVE AND PEACE WILL BE WITH YOU.

DAILY JOURNAL PROMPT

What do you want to
thank God for today?

Is there anything troubling you
that is disrupting your level of
hope or your faith today?

What scripture will you
focus on as a reminder of
God's promises?

What do you sense God
wants for you to remember
or know today?

COLOSSIANS 3:15

LET THE PEACE OF CHRIST RULE IN YOUR HEARTS, SINCE AS MEMBERS
OF ONE BODY YOU WERE CALLED TO PEACE. AND BE THANKFUL.

DAILY JOURNAL PROMPT

What do you feel most thankful for today?

Are there any issues that are troubling you where you need God's serenity?

What do you need God's courage and strength to change today?

What wisdom do you sense God is attempting to share with you or remind you of today?

ISAIAH 26:3

YOU WILL KEEP IN PERFECT PEACE THOSE WHOSE MINDS ARE STEADFAST, BECAUSE THEY TRUST IN YOU.

DAILY JOURNAL PROMPT

What do you want to thank God for today?

Is there anything troubling you that is disrupting your level of hope or your faith today?

What scripture will you focus on as a reminder of God's promises?

What do you sense God wants for you to remember or know today?

1 PETER 3:11

THEY MUST TURN FROM EVIL AND DO GOOD; THEY MUST SEEK PEACE AND PURSUE IT.

DAILY JOURNAL PROMPT

What do you feel most
thankful for today?

Are there any issues that are
troubling you where you need
God's serenity?

What do you need God's
courage and strength to
change today?

What wisdom do you sense
God is attempting to share
with you or remind you of
today?

ROMANS 5:1

THEREFORE, SINCE WE HAVE BEEN JUSTIFIED THROUGH FAITH,
WE HAVE PEACE WITH GOD THROUGH OUR LORD JESUS CHRIST,

DAILY JOURNAL PROMPT

What do you want to
thank God for today?

Is there anything troubling you
that is disrupting your level of
hope or your faith today?

What scripture will you
focus on as a reminder of
God's promises?

What do you sense God
wants for you to remember
or know today?

PROVERBS 16:7

WHEN THE LORD TAKES PLEASURE IN ANYONE'S WAY, HE CAUSES THEIR ENEMIES TO MAKE PEACE WITH THEM.

DAILY JOURNAL PROMPT

What do you feel most
thankful for today?

Are there any issues that are
troubling you where you need
God's serenity?

What do you need God's
courage and strength to
change today?

What wisdom do you sense
God is attempting to share
with you or remind you of
today?

MATTHEW 5:9

BLESSED ARE THE PEACEMAKERS, FOR THEY WILL BE CALLED CHILDREN OF GOD.

DAILY JOURNAL PROMPT

What do you want to
thank God for today?
_____
_____

Is there anything troubling you
that is disrupting your level of
hope or your faith today?
_____
_____

What scripture will you
focus on as a reminder of
God's promises?
_____
_____

What do you sense God
wants for you to remember
or know today?
_____
_____

2 THESSALONIANS 3:16

NOW MAY THE LORD OF PEACE HIMSELF GIVE YOU PEACE AT ALL
TIMES AND IN EVERY WAY. THE LORD BE WITH ALL OF YOU.

DAILY JOURNAL PROMPT

What do you feel most thankful for today?

Are there any issues that are troubling you where you need God's serenity?

What do you need God's courage and strength to change today?

What wisdom do you sense God is attempting to share with you or remind you of today?

EPHESIANS 6:15

AND WITH YOUR FEET FITTED WITH THE READINESS THAT COMES FROM THE GOSPEL OF PEACE.

DAILY JOURNAL PROMPT

What do you want to thank God for today?

Is there anything troubling you that is disrupting your level of hope or your faith today?

What scripture will you focus on as a reminder of God's promises?

What do you sense God wants for you to remember or know today?

PSALM 18:32

IT IS GOD WHO ARMS ME WITH STRENGTH AND KEEPS MY WAY SECURE.

DAILY JOURNAL PROMPT

What do you feel most
thankful for today?

Are there any issues that are
troubling you where you need
God's serenity?

What do you need God's
courage and strength to
change today?

What wisdom do you sense
God is attempting to share
with you or remind you of
today?

ROMANS 16:20

THE GOD OF PEACE WILL SOON CRUSH SATAN UNDER YOUR FEET. THE GRACE OF OUR LORD JESUS BE WITH YOU.

DAILY JOURNAL PROMPT

What do you want to thank God for today?

Is there anything troubling you that is disrupting your level of hope or your faith today?

What scripture will you focus on as a reminder of God's promises?

What do you sense God wants for you to remember or know today?

PHILIPPIANS 4:9

WHATEVER YOU HAVE LEARNED OR RECEIVED OR HEARD FROM ME, OR SEEN
IN ME—PUT IT INTO PRACTICE. AND THE GOD OF PEACE WILL BE WITH YOU.

DAILY JOURNAL PROMPT

What do you feel most thankful for today?

Are there any issues that are troubling you where you need God's serenity?

What do you need God's courage and strength to change today?

What wisdom do you sense God is attempting to share with you or remind you of today?

JOHN 14:27

PEACE I LEAVE WITH YOU; MY PEACE I GIVE TO YOU; NOT AS THE WORLD GIVES DO
I GIVE TO YOU. DO NOT LET YOUR HEART BE TROUBLED, NOR LET IT BE FEARFUL.

DAILY JOURNAL PROMPT

What do you want to
thank God for today?

Is there anything troubling you
that is disrupting your level of
hope or your faith today?

What scripture will you
focus on as a reminder of
God's promises?

What do you sense God
wants for you to remember
or know today?

PSALM 116:7

RETURN TO YOUR REST, O MY SOUL, FOR THE LORD HAS DEALT BOUNTIFULLY WITH YOU.

DAILY JOURNAL PROMPT

What do you feel most thankful for today?

Are there any issues that are troubling you where you need God's serenity?

What do you need God's courage and strength to change today?

What wisdom do you sense God is attempting to share with you or remind you of today?

1 CORINTHIANS 2:9

BUT JUST AS IT IS WRITTEN, "THINGS WHICH EYE HAS NOT SEEN AND EAR HAS NOT HEARD, AND WHICH HAVE NOT ENTERED THE HEART OF MAN, ALL THAT GOD HAS PREPARED FOR THOSE WHO LOVE HIM.

DAILY JOURNAL PROMPT

What do you want to
thank God for today?

Is there anything troubling you
that is disrupting your level of
hope or your faith today?

What scripture will you
focus on as a reminder of
God's promises?

What do you sense God
wants for you to remember
or know today?

ROMANS 8:6

THE MIND GOVERNED BY THE FLESH IS DEATH, BUT THE MIND GOVERNED BY THE SPIRIT IS LIFE AND PEACE.

DAILY JOURNAL PROMPT

What do you feel most thankful for today?	**Are there any issues that are troubling you where you need God's serenity?**
What do you need God's courage and strength to change today?	**What wisdom do you sense God is attempting to share with you or remind you of today?**

EPHESIANS 6:24

GRACE BE WITH ALL THOSE WHO LOVE OUR LORD JESUS CHRIST WITH INCORRUPTIBLE LOVE.

DAILY JOURNAL PROMPT

What do you want to thank God for today?	**Is there anything troubling you that is disrupting your level of hope or your faith today?**
What scripture will you focus on as a reminder of God's promises?	**What do you sense God wants for you to remember or know today?**

ISAIAH 12:2

SURELY GOD IS MY SALVATION; I WILL TRUST AND NOT BE AFRAID. THE LORD, THE
LORD HIMSELF, IS MY STRENGTH AND MY DEFENSE ; HE HAS BECOME MY SALVATION.

DAILY JOURNAL PROMPT

What do you feel most
thankful for today?

Are there any issues that are
troubling you where you need
God's serenity?

What do you need God's
courage and strength to
change today?

What wisdom do you sense
God is attempting to share
with you or remind you of
today?

PSALM 29:11

THE LORD GIVES STRENGTH TO HIS PEOPLE; THE LORD BLESSES HIS PEOPLE WITH PEACE.

DAILY JOURNAL PROMPT

What do you want to thank God for today?

Is there anything troubling you that is disrupting your level of hope or your faith today?

What scripture will you focus on as a reminder of God's promises?

What do you sense God wants for you to remember or know today?

HABAKKUK 3:19

THE SOVEREIGN LORD IS MY STRENGTH; HE MAKES MY FEET LIKE
THE FEET OF A DEER, HE ENABLES ME TO TREAD ON THE HEIGHTS.

DAILY JOURNAL PROMPT

What do you feel most
thankful for today?

Are there any issues that are
troubling you where you need
God's serenity?

What do you need God's
courage and strength to
change today?

What wisdom do you sense
God is attempting to share
with you or remind you of
today?

1 THESSALONIANS 5:15

MAKE SURE THAT NOBODY PAYS BACK WRONG FOR WRONG, BUT ALWAYS
STRIVE TO DO WHAT IS GOOD FOR EACH OTHER AND FOR EVERYONE ELSE.

DAILY JOURNAL PROMPT

What do you want to thank God for today?

Is there anything troubling you that is disrupting your level of hope or your faith today?

What scripture will you focus on as a reminder of God's promises?

What do you sense God wants for you to remember or know today?

1 PETER 5:7

CAST ALL YOUR ANXIETY ON HIM BECAUSE HE CARES FOR YOU.

DAILY JOURNAL PROMPT

What do you feel most
thankful for today?

Are there any issues that are
troubling you where you need
God's serenity?

What do you need God's
courage and strength to
change today?

What wisdom do you sense
God is attempting to share
with you or remind you of
today?

PROVERBS 12:20

DECEIT IS IN THE HEARTS OF THOSE WHO PLOT EVIL, BUT THOSE WHO PROMOTE PEACE HAVE JOY.

DAILY JOURNAL PROMPT

What do you want to thank God for today?

Is there anything troubling you that is disrupting your level of hope or your faith today?

What scripture will you focus on as a reminder of God's promises?

What do you sense God wants for you to remember or know today?

ROMANS 12:18

IF IT IS POSSIBLE, AS FAR AS IT DEPENDS ON YOU, LIVE AT PEACE WITH EVERYONE.

DAILY JOURNAL PROMPT

What do you feel most
thankful for today?

Are there any issues that are
troubling you where you need
God's serenity?

What do you need God's
courage and strength to
change today?

What wisdom do you sense
God is attempting to share
with you or remind you of
today?

GALATIANS 5:1
FOR FREEDOM CHRIST HAS SET US FREE; STAND FIRM
THEREFORE, AND DO NOT SUBMIT AGAIN TO A YOKE OF SLAVERY.

DAILY JOURNAL PROMPT

What do you want to
thank God for today?

Is there anything troubling you
that is disrupting your level of
hope or your faith today?

What scripture will you
focus on as a reminder of
God's promises?

What do you sense God
wants for you to remember
or know today?

1 THESSALONIANS 5:11

THEREFORE ENCOURAGE ONE ANOTHER AND BUILD EACH OTHER UP, JUST AS IN FACT YOU ARE DOING.

DAILY JOURNAL PROMPT

What do you feel most
thankful for today?

Are there any issues that are
troubling you where you need
God's serenity?

What do you need God's
courage and strength to
change today?

What wisdom do you sense
God is attempting to share
with you or remind you of
today?

JAMES 3:18

PEACEMAKERS WHO SOW IN PEACE REAP A HARVEST OF RIGHTEOUSNESS.

DAILY JOURNAL PROMPT

What do you want to thank God for today?

Is there anything troubling you that is disrupting your level of hope or your faith today?

What scripture will you focus on as a reminder of God's promises?

What do you sense God wants for you to remember or know today?

PSALMS 34:14

TURN FROM EVIL AND DO GOOD; SEEK PEACE AND PURSUE IT.

DAILY JOURNAL PROMPT

What do you feel most
thankful for today?

Are there any issues that are
troubling you where you need
God's serenity?

What do you need God's
courage and strength to
change today?

What wisdom do you sense
God is attempting to share
with you or remind you of
today?

ROMANS 14:19

LET US THEREFORE MAKE EVERY EFFORT TO DO WHAT LEADS TO PEACE AND TO MUTUAL EDIFICATION.

DAILY JOURNAL PROMPT

What do you want to
thank God for today?

Is there anything troubling you
that is disrupting your level of
hope or your faith today?

What scripture will you
focus on as a reminder of
God's promises?

What do you sense God
wants for you to remember
or know today?

PSALMS 85:8

I WILL LISTEN TO WHAT GOD THE LORD SAYS; HE PROMISES PEACE TO HIS
PEOPLE, HIS FAITHFUL SERVANTS— BUT LET THEM NOT TURN TO FOLLY.

DAILY JOURNAL PROMPT

What do you feel most thankful for today?

Are there any issues that are troubling you where you need God's serenity?

What do you need God's courage and strength to change today?

What wisdom do you sense God is attempting to share with you or remind you of today?

PSALMS 37:37

CONSIDER THE BLAMELESS, OBSERVE THE UPRIGHT; A FUTURE AWAITS THOSE WHO SEEK PEACE.

DAILY JOURNAL PROMPT

What do you want to
thank God for today?

Is there anything troubling you
that is disrupting your level of
hope or your faith today?

What scripture will you
focus on as a reminder of
God's promises?

What do you sense God
wants for you to remember
or know today?

PSALM 119:165

GREAT PEACE HAVE THOSE WHO LOVE YOUR LAW, AND NOTHING CAN MAKE THEM STUMBLE.

DAILY JOURNAL PROMPT

What do you feel most
thankful for today?

Are there any issues that are
troubling you where you need
God's serenity?

What do you need God's
courage and strength to
change today?

What wisdom do you sense
God is attempting to share
with you or remind you of
today?

JOHN 15:7

"IF YOU ABIDE IN ME, AND MY WORDS ABIDE IN YOU, ASK WHATEVER YOU WISH, AND IT WILL BE DONE FOR YOU."

DAILY JOURNAL PROMPT

What do you want to
thank God for today?

Is there anything troubling you
that is disrupting your level of
hope or your faith today?

What scripture will you
focus on as a reminder of
God's promises?

What do you sense God
wants for you to remember
or know today?

PSALM 42:11

WHY, MY SOUL, ARE YOU DOWNCAST? WHY SO DISTURBED WITHIN ME?
PUT YOUR HOPE IN GOD, OR I WILL YET PRAISE HIM, MY SAVIOR AND MY GOD.

DAILY JOURNAL PROMPT

What do you feel most
thankful for today?

Are there any issues that are
troubling you where you need
God's serenity?

What do you need God's
courage and strength to
change today?

What wisdom do you sense
God is attempting to share
with you or remind you of
today?

ISAIAH 40:31

BUT THOSE WHO HOPE IN THE LORD WILL RENEW THEIR STRENGTH. THEY WILL SOAR ON WINGS
LIKE EAGLES; THEY WILL RUN AND NOT GROW WEARY. THEY WILL WALK AND NOT BE FAINT.

DAILY JOURNAL PROMPT

What do you want to
thank God for today?

Is there anything troubling you
that is disrupting your level of
hope or your faith today?

What scripture will you
focus on as a reminder of
God's promises?

What do you sense God
wants for you to remember
or know today?

PSALM 32:7
YOU ARE A HIDING PLACE FOR ME; YOU PRESERVE ME FROM TROUBLE;
YOU SURROUND ME WITH SHOUTS OF DELIVERANCE. SELAH.

DAILY JOURNAL PROMPT

What do you feel most
thankful for today?

Are there any issues that are
troubling you where you need
God's serenity?

What do you need God's
courage and strength to
change today?

What wisdom do you sense
God is attempting to share
with you or remind you of
today?

PSALM 28:7-8

7 THE LORD IS MY STRENGTH AND MY SHIELD; MY HEART TRUSTS IN HIM, AND HE
HELPS ME. MY HEART LEAPS FOR JOY, AND WITH MY SONG I PRAISE HIM. 8 THE LORD
IS THE STRENGTH OF HIS PEOPLE, A FORTRESS OF SALVATION FOR HIS ANOINTED ONE.

DAILY JOURNAL PROMPT

What do you want to thank God for today?

Is there anything troubling you that is disrupting your level of hope or your faith today?

What scripture will you focus on as a reminder of God's promises?

What do you sense God wants for you to remember or know today?

ROMANS 5:3-4

NOT ONLY SO, BUT WE ALSO GLORY IN OUR SUFFERINGS, BECAUSE WE KNOW THAT SUFFERING PRODUCES PERSEVERANCE; PERSEVERANCE, CHARACTER; AND CHARACTER, HOPE.

DAILY JOURNAL PROMPT

What do you feel most
thankful for today?

Are there any issues that are
troubling you where you need
God's serenity?

What do you need God's
courage and strength to
change today?

What wisdom do you sense
God is attempting to share
with you or remind you of
today?

LUKE 10:19

"BEHOLD, I HAVE GIVEN YOU AUTHORITY TO TREAD ON SERPENTS AND SCORPIONS, AND OVER ALL THE POWER OF THE ENEMY, AND NOTHING SHALL HURT YOU."

DAILY JOURNAL PROMPT

What do you want to thank God for today?

Is there anything troubling you that is disrupting your level of hope or your faith today?

What scripture will you focus on as a reminder of God's promises?

What do you sense God wants for you to remember or know today?

HEBREWS 10:23

LET US HOLD UNSWERVINGLY TO THE HOPE WE PROFESS, FOR HE WHO PROMISED IS FAITHFUL.

DAILY JOURNAL PROMPT

What do you feel most thankful for today?

Are there any issues that are troubling you where you need God's serenity?

What do you need God's courage and strength to change today?

What wisdom do you sense God is attempting to share with you or remind you of today?

PSALM 31:24

BE STRONG AND TAKE HEART, ALL YOU WHO HOPE IN THE LORD.

DAILY JOURNAL PROMPT

What do you want to thank God for today?

Is there anything troubling you that is disrupting your level of hope or your faith today?

What scripture will you focus on as a reminder of God's promises?

What do you sense God wants for you to remember or know today?

MARK 9:23

" 'IF YOU CAN'?" SAID JESUS. "EVERYTHING IS POSSIBLE FOR ONE WHO BELIEVES."

DAILY JOURNAL PROMPT

What do you feel most
thankful for today?

Are there any issues that are
troubling you where you need
God's serenity?

What do you need God's
courage and strength to
change today?

What wisdom do you sense
God is attempting to share
with you or remind you of
today?

JOHN 10:10

"THE THIEF COMES ONLY TO STEAL AND KILL AND DESTROY. I CAME THAT THEY MAY HAVE LIFE AND HAVE IT ABUNDANTLY."

DAILY JOURNAL PROMPT

What do you want to thank God for today?

Is there anything troubling you that is disrupting your level of hope or your faith today?

What scripture will you focus on as a reminder of God's promises?

What do you sense God wants for you to remember or know today?

EPHESIANS 1:18

I PRAY THAT THE EYES OF YOUR HEART MAY BE ENLIGHTENED IN ORDER THAT
YOU MAY KNOW THE HOPE TO WHICH HE HAS CALLED YOU, THE RICHES OF HIS
GLORIOUS INHERITANCE IN HIS HOLY PEOPLE

DAILY JOURNAL PROMPT

What do you feel most
thankful for today?

Are there any issues that are
troubling you where you need
God's serenity?

What do you need God's
courage and strength to
change today?

What wisdom do you sense
God is attempting to share
with you or remind you of
today?

PHILIPPIANS 1:6

BEING CONFIDENT OF THIS, THAT HE WHO BEGAN A GOOD WORK IN YOU
WILL CARRY IT ON TO COMPLETION UNTIL THE DAY OF CHRIST JESUS.

DAILY JOURNAL PROMPT

What do you want to thank God for today?

Is there anything troubling you that is disrupting your level of hope or your faith today?

What scripture will you focus on as a reminder of God's promises?

What do you sense God wants for you to remember or know today?

PSALM 107:20

HE SENT OUT HIS WORD AND HEALED THEM, AND DELIVERED THEM FROM THEIR DESTRUCTION.

DAILY JOURNAL PROMPT

What do you feel most
thankful for today?

Are there any issues that are
troubling you where you need
God's serenity?

What do you need God's
courage and strength to
change today?

What wisdom do you sense
God is attempting to share
with you or remind you of
today?

1 TIMOTHY 4:10

"THAT IS WHY WE LABOR AND STRIVE, BECAUSE WE HAVE PUT OUR HOPE IN THE LIVING GOD, WHO IS THE SAVIOR OF ALL PEOPLE, AND ESPECIALLY OF THOSE WHO BELIEVE."

DAILY JOURNAL PROMPT

What do you want to
thank God for today?

Is there anything troubling you
that is disrupting your level of
hope or your faith today?

What scripture will you
focus on as a reminder of
God's promises?

What do you sense God
wants for you to remember
or know today?

PROVERBS 24:14

KNOW ALSO THAT WISDOM IS LIKE HONEY FOR YOU: IF YOU FIND IT, THERE
IS A FUTURE HOPE FOR YOU, AND YOUR HOPE WILL NOT BE CUT OFF.

DAILY JOURNAL PROMPT

What do you feel most
thankful for today?

Are there any issues that are
troubling you where you need
God's serenity?

What do you need God's
courage and strength to
change today?

What wisdom do you sense
God is attempting to share
with you or remind you of
today?

EPHESIANS 4:4

THERE IS ONE BODY AND ONE SPIRIT, JUST AS YOU
WERE CALLED TO ONE HOPE WHEN YOU WERE CALLED.

DAILY JOURNAL PROMPT

What do you want to thank God for today?

Is there anything troubling you that is disrupting your level of hope or your faith today?

What scripture will you focus on as a reminder of God's promises?

What do you sense God wants for you to remember or know today?

ROMANS 5:5

AND HOPE DOES NOT PUT US TO SHAME, BECAUSE GOD'S LOVE HAS BEEN POURED
OUT INTO OUR HEARTS THROUGH THE HOLY SPIRIT, WHO HAS BEEN GIVEN TO US.

DAILY JOURNAL PROMPT

What do you feel most
thankful for today?

Are there any issues that are
troubling you where you need
God's serenity?

What do you need God's
courage and strength to
change today?

What wisdom do you sense
God is attempting to share
with you or remind you of
today?

PSALM 33:22

MAY YOUR UNFAILING LOVE BE WITH US, LORD, EVEN AS WE PUT OUR HOPE IN YOU.

DAILY JOURNAL PROMPT

What do you want to thank God for today?

Is there anything troubling you that is disrupting your level of hope or your faith today?

What scripture will you focus on as a reminder of God's promises?

What do you sense God wants for you to remember or know today?

PHILIPPIANS 4:8

FINALLY, BROTHERS, WHATEVER IS TRUE, WHATEVER IS HONORABLE, WHATEVER IS JUST,
WHATEVER IS PURE, WHATEVER IS LOVELY, WHATEVER IS COMMENDABLE, IF THERE IS ANY
EXCELLENCE, IF THERE IS ANYTHING WORTHY OF PRAISE, THINK ABOUT THESE THINGS.

DAILY JOURNAL PROMPT

What do you feel most
thankful for today?

Are there any issues that are
troubling you where you need
God's serenity?

What do you need God's
courage and strength to
change today?

What wisdom do you sense
God is attempting to share
with you or remind you of
today?

MICAH 7:7
BUT AS FOR ME, I WATCH IN HOPE FOR THE LORD, I
WAIT FOR GOD MY SAVIOR; MY GOD WILL HEAR ME.

DAILY JOURNAL PROMPT

What do you want to
thank God for today?

Is there anything troubling you
that is disrupting your level of
hope or your faith today?

What scripture will you
focus on as a reminder of
God's promises?

What do you sense God
wants for you to remember
or know today?

AMOS 9:14

AND I WILL BRING MY PEOPLE ISRAEL BACK FROM EXILE. "THEY WILL REBUILD THE
RUINED CITIES AND LIVE IN THEM. THEY WILL PLANT VINEYARDS AND DRINK THEIR WINE;
THEY WILL MAKE GARDENS AND EAT THEIR FRUIT.

DAILY JOURNAL PROMPT

What do you feel most
thankful for today?

Are there any issues that are
troubling you where you need
God's serenity?

What do you need God's
courage and strength to
change today?

What wisdom do you sense
God is attempting to share
with you or remind you of
today?

GALATIANS 6:1

BROTHERS AND SISTERS, IF SOMEONE IS CAUGHT IN A SIN, YOU WHO LIVE BY THE SPIRIT SHOULD
RESTORE THAT PERSON GENTLY. BUT WATCH YOURSELVES, OR YOU ALSO MAY BE TEMPTED.

DAILY JOURNAL PROMPT

What do you want to
thank God for today?

Is there anything troubling you
that is disrupting your level of
hope or your faith today?

What scripture will you
focus on as a reminder of
God's promises?

What do you sense God
wants for you to remember
or know today?

HOSEA 6:1

COME, LET US RETURN TO THE LORD. HE HAS TORN US TO PIECES BUT HE
WILL HEAL US; HE HAS INJURED US BUT HE WILL BIND UP OUR WOUNDS.

DAILY JOURNAL PROMPT

What do you feel most thankful for today?

Are there any issues that are troubling you where you need God's serenity?

What do you need God's courage and strength to change today?

What wisdom do you sense God is attempting to share with you or remind you of today?

ISAIAH 61:7

INSTEAD OF YOUR SHAME YOU WILL RECEIVE A DOUBLE PORTION, AND INSTEAD OF
DISGRACE YOU WILL REJOICE IN YOUR INHERITANCE. AND SO YOU WILL INHERIT A
DOUBLE PORTION IN YOUR LAND, AND EVERLASTING JOY WILL BE YOURS.

DAILY JOURNAL PROMPT

What do you want to
thank God for today?

Is there anything troubling you
that is disrupting your level of
hope or your faith today?

What scripture will you
focus on as a reminder of
God's promises?

What do you sense God
wants for you to remember
or know today?

JEREMIAH 17:14

HEAL ME, LORD, AND I WILL BE HEALED; SAVE ME AND I
WILL BE SAVED, FOR YOU ARE THE ONE I PRAISE.

DAILY JOURNAL PROMPT

What do you feel most thankful for today?	Are there any issues that are troubling you where you need God's serenity?

What do you need God's courage and strength to change today?	What wisdom do you sense God is attempting to share with you or remind you of today?

JEREMIAH 30:17

HEAL ME, LORD, AND I WILL BE HEALED; SAVE ME AND I WILL BE SAVED, FOR YOU ARE THE ONE I PRAISE.

DAILY JOURNAL PROMPT

What do you want to
thank God for today?

Is there anything troubling you
that is disrupting your level of
hope or your faith today?

What scripture will you
focus on as a reminder of
God's promises?

What do you sense God
wants for you to remember
or know today?

JOB 42:10

AFTER JOB HAD PRAYED FOR HIS FRIENDS, THE LORD RESTORED HIS
FORTUNES AND GAVE HIM TWICE AS MUCH AS HE HAD BEFORE.

DAILY JOURNAL PROMPT

What do you feel most thankful for today?	Are there any issues that are troubling you where you need God's serenity?

What do you need God's courage and strength to change today?	What wisdom do you sense God is attempting to share with you or remind you of today?

1 PETER 5:10

AND THE GOD OF ALL GRACE, WHO CALLED YOU TO HIS ETERNAL GLORY IN
CHRIST, AFTER YOU HAVE SUFFERED A LITTLE WHILE, WILL HIMSELF
RESTORE YOU AND MAKE YOU STRONG, FIRM AND STEADFAST.

DAILY JOURNAL PROMPT

What do you want to
thank God for today?

Is there anything troubling you
that is disrupting your level of
hope or your faith today?

What scripture will you
focus on as a reminder of
God's promises?

What do you sense God
wants for you to remember
or know today?

1 JOHN 5:4

FOR EVERYONE BORN OF GOD OVERCOMES THE WORLD. THIS IS
THE VICTORY THAT HAS OVERCOME THE WORLD, EVEN OUR FAITH.

DAILY JOURNAL PROMPT

What do you feel most thankful for today?

Are there any issues that are troubling you where you need God's serenity?

What do you need God's courage and strength to change today?

What wisdom do you sense God is attempting to share with you or remind you of today?

2 CORINTHIANS 5:17
THEREFORE, IF ANYONE IS IN CHRIST, THE NEW CREATION
HAS COME: THE OLD HAS GONE, THE NEW IS HERE!

DAILY JOURNAL PROMPT

What do you want to
thank God for today?

Is there anything troubling you
that is disrupting your level of
hope or your faith today?

What scripture will you
focus on as a reminder of
God's promises?

What do you sense God
wants for you to remember
or know today?

JOHN 14:1

DO NOT LET YOUR HEARTS BE TROUBLED. YOU BELIEVE IN GOD; BELIEVE ALSO IN ME.

DAILY JOURNAL PROMPT

What do you feel most
thankful for today?

Are there any issues that are
troubling you where you need
God's serenity?

What do you need God's
courage and strength to
change today?

What wisdom do you sense
God is attempting to share
with you or remind you of
today?

MARK 11:24

THEREFORE I TELL YOU, WHATEVER YOU ASK FOR IN PRAYER,
BELIEVE THAT YOU HAVE RECEIVED IT, AND IT WILL BE YOURS.

DAILY JOURNAL PROMPT

What do you want to thank God for today?

Is there anything troubling you that is disrupting your level of hope or your faith today?

What scripture will you focus on as a reminder of God's promises?

What do you sense God wants for you to remember or know today?

MATTHEW 11:28
COME TO ME, ALL YOU WHO ARE WEARY AND BURDENED, AND I WILL GIVE YOU REST.

DAILY JOURNAL PROMPT

What do you feel most
thankful for today?

Are there any issues that are
troubling you where you need
God's serenity?

What do you need God's
courage and strength to
change today?

What wisdom do you sense
God is attempting to share
with you or remind you of
today?

PSALMS 51:12

RESTORE TO ME THE JOY OF YOUR SALVATION AND GRANT ME A WILLING SPIRIT, TO SUSTAIN ME.

DAILY JOURNAL PROMPT

What do you want to
thank God for today?

Is there anything troubling you
that is disrupting your level of
hope or your faith today?

What scripture will you
focus on as a reminder of
God's promises?

What do you sense God
wants for you to remember
or know today?

ROMANS 15:5

MAY THE GOD WHO GIVES ENDURANCE AND ENCOURAGEMENT GIVE YOU THE
SAME ATTITUDE OF MIND TOWARD EACH OTHER THAT CHRIST JESUS HAD.

DAILY JOURNAL PROMPT

What do you feel most
thankful for today?

Are there any issues that are
troubling you where you need
God's serenity?

What do you need God's
courage and strength to
change today?

What wisdom do you sense
God is attempting to share
with you or remind you of
today?

JAMES 4:7

SUBMIT YOURSELVES THEREFORE TO GOD. RESIST THE DEVIL, AND HE WILL FLEE FROM YOU.

DAILY JOURNAL PROMPT

What do you want to
thank God for today?

Is there anything troubling you
that is disrupting your level of
hope or your faith today?

What scripture will you
focus on as a reminder of
God's promises?

What do you sense God
wants for you to remember
or know today?

PSALM 121:1-2

I LIFT UP MY EYES TO THE MOUNTAINS—WHERE DOES MY HELP COME FROM? MY
HELP COMES FROM THE LORD, THE MAKER OF HEAVEN AND EARTH.

DAILY JOURNAL PROMPT

What do you feel most thankful for today?

Are there any issues that are troubling you where you need God's serenity?

What do you need God's courage and strength to change today?

What wisdom do you sense God is attempting to share with you or remind you of today?

NEHEMIAH 8:10
DO NOT GRIEVE, FOR THE JOY OF THE LORD IS YOUR STRENGTH.

DAILY JOURNAL PROMPT

What do you want to thank God for today?	Is there anything troubling you that is disrupting your level of hope or your faith today?
What scripture will you focus on as a reminder of God's promises?	What do you sense God wants for you to remember or know today?

EXODUS 15:2

THE LORD IS MY STRENGTH AND MY SONG; HE HAS GIVEN ME VICTORY. THIS IS MY GOD, AND I WILL PRAISE HIM——MY FATHER'S GOD, AND I WILL EXALT HIM.

DAILY JOURNAL PROMPT

What do you feel most
thankful for today?

Are there any issues that are
troubling you where you need
God's serenity?

What do you need God's
courage and strength to
change today?

What wisdom do you sense
God is attempting to share
with you or remind you of
today?

JOSHUA 1:9

BE STRONG AND COURAGEOUS; DO NOT BE FRIGHTENED AND DO NOT BE
DISMAYED. FOR THE LORD YOUR GOD IS WITH YOU WHEREVER YOU GO.

DAILY JOURNAL PROMPT

What do you want to thank God for today?	Is there anything troubling you that is disrupting your level of hope or your faith today?

What scripture will you focus on as a reminder of God's promises?	What do you sense God wants for you to remember or know today?

EPHESIANS 6:10

FINALLY, BE STRONG IN THE LORD AND IN HIS MIGHTY POWER.

Made in the USA
Middletown, DE
02 September 2024

60238647R00106